United States Government Accountability Office

# Report to Congressional Committees

I0425873

February 2012

# DEFENSE WORKFORCE

## DOD Needs to Better Oversee In-sourcing Data and Align In-sourcing Efforts with Strategic Workforce Plans

**GAO**

Accountability ★ Integrity ★ Reliability

# DEFENSE WORKFORCE

## DOD Needs to Better Oversee In-sourcing Data and Align In-sourcing Efforts with Strategic Workforce Plans

**GAO**
Accountability * Integrity * Reliability

# Highlights

Highlights of GAO-12-319, a report to congressional committees

## Why GAO Did This Study

The Department of Defense (DOD) relies on contractors for varied functions, and obligated about $200 billion in fiscal year 2010 for contracted services. In-sourcing—moving contracted work to performance by DOD employees—has been one tool through which DOD managed its workforce. The National Defense Authorization Act for Fiscal Year 2011 required DOD to report on its fiscal year 2010 in-sourcing decisions and required GAO to assess DOD's report. The act required DOD to report, for each decision, the agency or service involved, the basis and rationale for the decision, and the number of contractor employees in-sourced. GAO assessed the report against these requirements and examined how DOD prepared the report and assured itself of the data's reliability, and the extent the in-sourcing actions were aligned with DOD's strategic workforce plans. GAO reviewed the in-sourcing report, examined in-sourcing guidance, reviewed DOD's recent strategic workforce plans, and interviewed appropriate department officials.

## What GAO Recommends

GAO recommends that, for future in-sourcing actions, DOD (1) issue guidance to components on verifying in-sourcing data, and (2) better align in-sourcing data with strategic workforce plans and establish metrics to measure progress against in-sourcing goals. DOD partially concurred with the recommendations, but noted that the challenges identified in GAO's report are not unique to in-sourcing. GAO agrees, but believes actions are necessary to improve oversight of DOD's in-sourcing.

View GAO-12-319. For more information, contact Brenda S. Farrell at (202) 512-3604 or farrellb@gao.gov or Belva M. Martin at (202) 512-4841 or martinb@gao.gov.

## What GAO Found

DOD reported on two of three issues required by law: the component involved with each of its fiscal year 2010 in-sourcing actions and the rationale for each action. However, DOD did not report the number of contractor employees whose functions were in-sourced, because, DOD officials said, the department does not have these data. Specifically, the department noted, in its report to Congress, that it contracts for services and does not hire individual contractor employees. Instead, DOD reported the number of new civilian authorizations created due to in-sourcing. Congress has separately required DOD to report the number of contractor employees performing services for DOD, expressed as full-time equivalents, as part of its inventory of activities performed under contracts for services. In its in-sourcing report, DOD said that efforts to comply with this additional requirement may in the future help inform the number of contractor full-time equivalents in-sourced.

The Office of the Under Secretary of Defense for Personnel and Readiness (OUSD (P&R)) requested information from DOD components on fiscal year 2010 in-sourcing actions to produce its report, and the military departments and OUSD (P&R) took varying, and in some instances limited, approaches to ensuring the data's reliability. Additionally, some of the commands GAO contacted made errors in reporting in-sourcing data. For example, 348 of 354 new in-sourcing authorizations by the Navy's Fleet Forces Command were categorized as inherently governmental when they should have been categorized as exempt from private sector performance for continuity of infrastructure operations. Federal internal control standards state that data verification helps provide management with reasonable assurance of achieving agency objectives, including compliance with laws. Without accurate data, decision-makers in DOD and Congress may not have reliable information to help manage and oversee DOD in-sourcing.

While the mandate did not require the in-sourcing report to align with DOD's strategic workforce plans, it was unclear to what extent the in-sourcing actions aligned with DOD's plan due to differences in the types of data used in the in-sourcing report and the most recent workforce plan, and the absence of metrics to measure the in-sourcing goal established in the plan. DOD took some steps toward aligning these efforts, such as establishing a goal for in-sourcing in its most recent strategic workforce plan, which was issued in March 2010. Additionally, OUSD (P&R) officials said that the in-sourcing actions furthered DOD's strategic workforce objectives, but acknowledged they had not established metrics to measure against the in-sourcing goal—which was to, among other things, optimize the department's workforce mix to maintain readiness and operational capability and ensure inherently governmental positions were performed by government employees. Additionally, the strategic workforce plans coded jobs by occupational series, such as budget analyst, while the in-sourcing report used function codes indicating broad areas of work, such as logistics. DOD officials told GAO there is no crosswalk between the two. GAO has previously reported that strategic workforce planning includes aligning human capital programs with programmatic goals. Without metrics and due to the differences in the data used, DOD and Congress may have limited insight on the extent to which in-sourcing actions met strategic workforce goals.

_____ United States Government Accountability Office

# Contents

**Abbreviations**

| | |
|---|---|
| DOD | Department of Defense |
| FY | fiscal year |
| NDAA | National Defense Authorization Act |
| OSD | Office of the Secretary of Defense |
| OUSD | Office of the Under Secretary of Defense |
| P&R | Personnel and Readiness |

United States Government Accountability Office
Washington, DC 20548

February 9, 2012

Congressional Committees

The Department of Defense (DOD) relies on contractors to perform functions as varied as professional and management support, information technology support, and weapon system and intelligence support, and in fiscal year 2010, DOD obligated about $200 billion for contracted services. Contracting for services can offer benefits and flexibility to DOD, but our prior work has also shown that reliance on contractors to support core missions can place the government at risk of transferring governmental responsibilities to contractors.[1] Further, we have previously reported that having the right number of civilian personnel with the right skills is critical to achieving DOD's mission.[2] In-sourcing—moving work performed by contractors to performance by DOD employees[3]—is one tool through which DOD can manage its total force (which includes DOD civilians, active and reserve military personnel, and contractors) and help ensure it has the necessary capabilities in its DOD civilian workforce to perform key functions and reduce the risk of over-reliance on its contractor workforce. Managing the total force through strategic workforce planning helps organizations such as DOD determine if they have the appropriate total workforce balance with the necessary skills and competencies to achieve their strategic goals.

---

[1] See, for example, GAO, *High-Risk Series: An Update*, GAO-11-278 (Washington, D.C.: February 2011); *Defense Management: DOD Needs to Reexamine Its Extensive Reliance on Contractors and Continue to Improve Management and Oversight*, GAO-08-572T (Washington, D.C.: Mar. 11, 2008), and Defense *Acquisitions: DOD's Increased Reliance on Service Contractors Exacerbates Long-standing Challenges*, GAO-08-621T (Washington, D.C.: Jan. 23, 2008).

[2] See, for example, GAO, *DOD Civilian Personnel: Competency Gap Analyses and Other Actions Needed to Enhance DOD's Strategic Workforce Plans*, GAO-11-827T (Washington, D.C.: July 14, 2011) and *Human Capital: Opportunities Exist to Build on Recent Progress to Strengthen DOD's Civilian Human Capital Strategic Plan*, GAO-09-235 (Washington, D.C.: Feb. 10, 2009).

[3] DOD defines in-sourcing as the conversion of any currently contracted service or function to DOD civilian or military performance (Deputy Secretary of Defense, *In-sourcing Contracted Services—Implementation Guidance*, May 28, 2009). However, for the purposes of this report we refer only to conversion to civilian, rather than military, performance.

In April 2009, the Secretary of Defense announced his intent to reduce the department's reliance on contractors through in-sourcing, stating that the department's goal was to hire as many as 13,000 new civil servants in fiscal year 2010 to replace contractors and up to 30,000 new civil servants in place of contractors over a 5-year period.

The National Defense Authorization Act for Fiscal Year 2011 (FY11 NDAA) required DOD to report to the congressional defense committees not later than March 31, 2011, on its fiscal year 2010 in-sourcing decisions.[4] Specifically, the act required the department to report, for each in-sourcing decision, (1) the agency or service of the department involved in the decision, (2) the basis and rationale for the decision, and (3) the number of contractor employees whose functions were converted to performance by DOD civilian employees. DOD submitted its report to the congressional armed services committees on September 7, 2011, and DOD officials told us the department submitted the report to the congressional appropriations committees on either September 7 or 8, 2011.

The act also required that we assess DOD's report within 120 days of the report's issuance.[5] This report addresses the extent to which DOD reported on its fiscal year 2010 in-sourcing decisions as required by the act. On the basis of congressional interest, we also address how DOD prepared its report on fiscal year 2010 in-sourcing decisions and the extent to which it assured itself of the data's reliability, and the extent to which DOD's fiscal year 2010 in-sourcing decisions were aligned with the department's recent strategic workforce plans.

To evaluate the extent to which DOD reported on its fiscal year 2010 in-sourcing decisions, we reviewed DOD's report and compared it with the reporting requirements specified in the legislation. We also met with officials in the Office of the Under Secretary of Defense for Personnel and Readiness (OUSD (P&R)) responsible for preparing the report, and representatives from each of the three military departments as well as select major commands to understand the report's underlying data. We focused our work for this and the remainder of our objectives on the

---

[4] The Ike Skelton National Defense Authorization Act for Fiscal Year 2011, Pub. L. No. 111-383, §323(c) (1) (2011).

[5] Pub. L. No. 111-383 § 323(c) (2) (2011).

military departments because together they constituted the majority of in-sourcing actions in fiscal year 2010. For the purposes of this review, we selected a non-probability sample of commands from each military service, which included at a minimum the largest two commands in each service by volume of in-sourcing actions in fiscal year 2010. The sample of commands is not generalizable to all military department major commands.

To determine the process DOD used to prepare the report and the extent to which the Office of the Secretary of Defense (OSD) and the military departments assured themselves of the reliability of the data, we reviewed our prior work on standards for internal control in the federal government.[6] We also reviewed DOD-issued guidance on the in-sourcing process, and met with officials in OUSD (P&R) responsible for preparing the report, as well as representatives of each of the three military departments responsible for compiling data for the report. We analyzed the data contained in the report to identify patterns in the in-sourcing actions of the military departments, and met with representatives of each military department and the selected major commands to identify the reasons for those patterns. We used these data to portray the distribution of in-sourcing actions across the military departments and other DOD agencies, as well as the distribution of in-sourcing rationales in the military services and within certain major commands. Although we found issues with some of the command-level data, such as some erroneously reported in-sourcing rationales, and are making a recommendation to this effect, we found the data to be sufficiently reliable for the purposes of providing broad percentages about in-sourcing actions.

To determine the extent to which DOD's fiscal year 2010 in-sourcing decisions were aligned with the department's recent strategic workforce plans, we reviewed DOD guidance on in-sourcing implementation and our prior work on strategic workforce planning, as well as Office of Personnel Management standards for assessing human capital planning. In addition, we compared information reflecting DOD's fiscal year 2010 in-sourcing decisions with its fiscal year 2009 update to its 2006-2010 strategic

---

[6] GAO, *Standards for Internal Control in the Federal Government*, GAO/AIMD-00-21.3.1 (Washington, D.C.: November 1999).

workforce plans.[7] We also interviewed officials in OUSD (P&R) responsible for preparing both the in-sourcing report and the strategic workforce plans, as well as officials in the Office of the Under Secretary of Defense for Acquisition, Technology, and Logistics' Office of Human Capital Initiatives, to determine what steps were taken to align in-sourcing efforts with strategic workforce plans.

We conducted this performance audit from May 2011 to February 2012 in accordance with generally accepted government auditing standards. Those standards require that we plan and perform the audit to obtain sufficient, appropriate evidence to provide a reasonable basis for our findings and conclusions based on our audit objectives. We believe that the evidence obtained provides a reasonable basis for our findings and conclusions based on our audit objectives. We discuss our scope and methodology in more detail in appendix I.

## Background

Beginning with the National Defense Authorization Act for Fiscal Year 2006,[8] Congress required the Secretary of Defense to issue guidelines requiring DOD to consider using federal employees to perform work that was currently being performed or would otherwise be performed under DOD contracts. Under the guidelines, special consideration was given to contracts that had been performed by federal government employees on or after October 1, 1980, were associated with the performance of inherently governmental functions,[9] had not been awarded on a competitive basis, or were determined to be poorly performed due to excessive costs or inferior quality.[10]

---

[7] DOD, *Strategic Civilian Human Capital Plan (SCHCP) 2006-2010, Fiscal Year 2009 status report* (Mar. 31, 2010), and *DOD Strategic Human Capital Plan Update, The Defense Acquisition Workforce* (April 2010). OUSD (P&R) officials told us these were the strategic workforce plans in place at the time of the fiscal year 2010 in-sourcing actions.

[8] The National Defense Authorization Act for Fiscal Year 2006, Pub. L. No. 109-163, § 343 (2006).

[9] Inherently governmental functions include functions that require discretion in applying government authority or value judgments in making decisions for the government. The Federal Acquisition Regulation (FAR) provides examples of such functions, including the determination of agency policy, such as determining the content and application of regulations, or the determination of federal program priorities for budget requests. FAR § 7.503(c).

[10] Pub. L. No. 109-163, § 343 (a) (2) (2006).

The National Defense Authorization Act for Fiscal Year 2008 codified at section 2463 of title 10 of the United States Code (U.S. Code) revised the guidelines and procedures for use of civilian employees to perform DOD functions.[11] This section directed the Under Secretary of Defense for Personnel and Readiness (P&R) to devise and implement guidelines and procedures to ensure that consideration was given to using, on a regular basis, DOD civilian employees to perform new functions. In addition, the guidelines and procedures were to ensure that functions that were performed by contractors and could be performed by DOD civilian employees were given the same consideration. Congress also directed that the guidelines and procedures may not include any specific limitation or restriction on the number of functions or activities that may be converted to performance by DOD civilian employees. The act further provided that DOD may not conduct a public-private competition prior to in-sourcing such functions. The act also added a new section describing the functions that were to receive special consideration from DOD when considering the use of DOD civilian employees. Additionally, the act required special consideration be given to a new requirement that is similar to a function previously performed by DOD civilian employees or is a function closely associated with the performance of an inherently governmental function.[12]

The National Defense Authorization Act for Fiscal Year 2008 also amended section 2330a of title 10 of the U.S. Code. The act required DOD to compile and submit to Congress an annual inventory of the activities performed during the preceding fiscal year pursuant to contracts for services for or on behalf of DOD.[13] Among other things, the entry for an activity on the inventory had to include, for the fiscal year covered by such entry, the functions and missions performed by the contractor and the number of contractor employees (or its equivalent), paid for the

---

[11] The National Defense Authorization Act for Fiscal Year 2008, Pub. L. No. 110-181, § 324 (2008).

[12] Closely associated with inherently governmental functions are those that, while not inherently governmental, may approach the category because of the nature of the function, the manner in which the contractor performs the contract, or the manner in which the government administers performance under such a contract. The FAR provides examples of such functions, including services that involve or relate to the development of regulations, or services that involve or relate to budget preparation, including workload modeling, fact-finding, and should-cost analyses. FAR § 7.503(d).

[13] Pub. L. No. 110-181, § 807 (2008).

performance of the activity. The National Defense Authorization Act for Fiscal Year 2011 again amended section 2330a of title 10 of the U.S. Code. Among other things the act now requires DOD to report the number of contractor employees, expressed as full-time equivalents for direct labor, using direct labor hours and associated cost data collected from contractors (except that estimates may be used where such data is not available and cannot reasonably be made available in a timely manner for the purpose of the inventory).[14]

Section 2330a (e) of title 10 of the U.S. Code requires each Secretary of a military department or head of a defense agency to review this annual inventory for several purposes, one of which is to identify activities that should be considered for conversion to performance by DOD civilian employees pursuant to section 2463 of title 10 of the U.S. Code. In turn section 2463 requires the Secretary of Defense to make use of the 2330a inventory for the purpose of identifying functions that should be considered for performance by DOD civilian employees.[15]

Under DOD's policy for determining the appropriate mix of military and DOD civilians and contractor support, risk mitigation shall take precedence over cost savings when necessary to maintain appropriate control of government operations and missions.[16] This policy provides manpower mix criteria for assessing which functions warrant performance by military or civilian personnel due to their associated risks, and which functions will therefore be considered exempt from performance by contractor support.[17] DOD issued in-sourcing guidance in April 2008 and again in May 2009 to assist components in implementing these legislative

---

[14] Pub. L. No. 111-383, § 321 (2011).

[15] Pub. L. No. 110-181, § 324 (2008).

[16] DOD Instruction 1100.22, *Policy and Procedures for Determining Workforce Mix* (Apr. 12, 2010).

[17] Under DOD Instruction 1100.22, certain functions will meet DOD's criteria to be considered exempt from performance by the private sector, e.g., activities necessary to provide for the readiness and workforce management needs of DOD, maintain core capabilities and readiness, or mitigate operational risk. Some, but not all, functions identified as closely associated with inherently governmental functions will meet the criteria necessary to be deemed exempt functions by DOD.

requirements.[18] According to the May 2009 guidance, DOD components should first confirm that a particular mission requirement is still valid and enduring; that is, that DOD will have a continued need for the service being performed. If the requirement is still valid, the component should consider in-sourcing the function. If the component determined that the function under review was inherently governmental or exempt from private sector performance no cost analysis was required. Possible rationales to in-source include the following, according to the May 2009 in-sourcing guidance:

- The function is inherently governmental; that is, the function is so closely related to the public interest as to require performance by government employees.
- The function is exempt from private sector performance to support the readiness or workforce management needs of DOD. According to DOD's policy for determining the appropriate mix of military, DOD civilians, and contractor support, a function could be exempt from private sector performance for a variety of reasons, including functions exempt for career progression reasons, continuity of infrastructure operations, and mitigation of operational risk.
- The contract is for unauthorized personal services. Special authorization is required for DOD to engage in personal services contracts, which create a direct employer/employee relationship between the government and the contractor's personnel.
- There are problems with contract administration due to a lack of sufficiently trained and experienced officials available to manage and oversee the contract.

Other than in-sourcing, OUSD (P&R) officials told us that DOD may be able to address the above circumstances by, among other approaches, restructuring the contract or changing the way the contract is overseen. DOD's guidance does not require components to prepare cost estimates when they cite one of the above reasons as the basis for their in-sourcing decision.

---

[18] Deputy Security of Defense, *Implementation of Section 324 of the National Defense Authorization Act for Fiscal Year 2008—Guidelines and Procedures on In-sourcing New and Contracted-Out Functions* (Apr. 4, 2008) and *In-sourcing Contracted Services— Implementation Guidance* (May 28, 2009).

In situations in which none of the factors cited above are applicable, DOD's guidance instructs components to provide "special consideration" as discussed above, and if DOD civilians could perform the work, conduct a cost analysis to determine whether DOD civilians were the lowest-cost provider. According to a December 2009 in-sourcing plan submitted to Congress,[19] DOD based this requirement on section 129a of title 10 of the U.S. Code, which requires DOD to determine the least costly personnel consistent with military requirements and other needs of the department.[20] Thus, DOD components may also in-source for cost reasons when the work could otherwise be performed by a private contractor.

DOD stated in its fiscal year 2010 budget submission to Congress that it expected to save $900 million in fiscal year 2010 from in-sourcing. To support the in-sourcing initiative, in April 2009 the Office of the Under Secretary of Defense (Comptroller) issued a budget decision which decreased funding for support service contracts and increased funding for new civilian authorizations across DOD components.[21] In December 2009, DOD issued a report to Congress on its planned fiscal year 2010 in-sourcing efforts, stating that after component reviews, the department planned to create as many as 17,000 new civilian authorizations as a result of in-sourcing in fiscal year 2010.

In August 2010, the Secretary of Defense stated that he was not satisfied with the department's progress in reducing over-reliance on contractors. Representatives of OUSD (P&R) and the Office of the Under Secretary of Defense (Comptroller) told us that although DOD avoided $900 million in costs for contracted support services in fiscal year 2010 due to the budget decision to reduce funds associated with in-sourcing, total spending across all categories of service contracts increased in fiscal year 2010 by about $4.1 billion. To accelerate the process and achieve additional

---

[19] DOD, *Report to the Congressional Defense Committees on the Department of Defense's FY 2010 In-sourcing Initiative and Plans* (December 2009).

[20] 10 U.S.C. § 129a.

[21] This budget action, called Resource Management Decision 802, assumed a 40 percent savings from the in-sourcing actions, so that roughly 60 percent of the original funding for contracted services went toward new civilian authorizations, while the remainder was retained by the Comptroller as savings available for other purposes. Thus, DOD components were required to either find savings under in-sourcing or reduce the functions they performed, or both.

savings, the Secretary directed a 3-year reduction in funding for service support contracts categorized by DOD as contracted support services. He also directed a 3-year freeze on the level of DOD civilian authorizations at OSD, the defense agencies, and the Combatant Commands, and stated that with regard to in-sourcing, no more DOD civilian authorizations would be created after the then-current fiscal year to replace contractors. He also noted that some exceptions could be made for critical areas such as the acquisition workforce. Further, the statutory requirement to regularly consider in-sourcing contracted services remains in effect, and DOD officials told us that, accordingly, in-sourcing continues in the department, though on a more limited basis. See figure 1 for a timeline of key events related to DOD in-sourcing.

**Figure 1: Timeline of Selected In-sourcing Events**

| 2006 | March 2009 | April 2009 | May 2009 | August 2010 | January 2011 |
|---|---|---|---|---|---|
| FY06 NDAA requires DOD to consider using federal employees to perform currently contracted work. | President directs federal agencies to reduce reliance on contractors. | Secretary of Defense announces an initiative to reduce service contractors and hire civilians to perform the work. | DOD issues updated in-sourcing implementation guidance. | Secretary of Defense states he is not satisfied with DOD's progress reducing reliance on contractors. | FY11 NDAA requires DOD to submit a report to Congress on its FY10 in-sourcing decisions, and requires GAO to review DOD's report. |

Source: GAO analysis of laws, White House and DOD public statements, and DOD guidance

Additionally, section 115b of title 10 of the U.S. Code requires DOD to annually submit to the defense committees a strategic workforce plan to shape and improve its civilian workforce. Among other requirements, the plan is to include an assessment of the appropriate mix of military, civilian, and contractor personnel capabilities. OUSD (P&R) is responsible for developing and implementing the strategic plan in consultation with the Office of the Under Secretary of Defense for Acquisition, Technology, and Logistics.[22] Since 2001, we have listed federal human capital management, of which strategic workforce planning is a key part, as a governmentwide high-risk area.[23] Similarly, we have identified challenges

---

[22] 10 U.S.C. § 115b (a) (2).

[23] GAO-11-278.

GAO-12-319 DOD In-sourcing Report

with having a sufficient number of adequately trained acquisition and contract oversight personnel as a factor in continuing to identify DOD contract management as a DOD-specific high-risk area.

## DOD's September 2011 In-sourcing Report Addressed Two of the Three Mandated Requirements

DOD's September 2011 in-sourcing report addressed the legislative requirements to report the service or agency involved with each of its fiscal year 2010 in-sourcing actions and the rationale for each action, but did not report the number of contractor employees whose functions were in-sourced, as specified in the act. DOD stated that it could not report the number of contractor employees because it contracts for services, rather than hiring contractor employees directly. An OUSD (P&R) official noted that one of the data elements Congress has required DOD to include in its annual inventories of contracted services is the number of contractor employees, expressed as full-time equivalents, that performed each activity,[24] and DOD is in the process of implementing a revised approach to collect these data directly from contractors.

### Service or Agency Information

DOD's report identified nearly 17,000 newly created civilian authorizations[25] as a result of in-sourcing actions in fiscal year 2010, and for each of these new authorizations, the department identified the DOD component involved with the decision.[26] For example, DOD reported that 42 percent of the new authorizations were established in the Army; 28 percent in the Air Force; 16 percent in the Department of the Navy (including the Marine Corps);[27] and 14 percent in other DOD agencies. The report also in many cases identified the major command,

---

[24] 10 U.S.C. § 2330a (c) (2) (E).

[25] DOD's in-sourcing report gives slightly different figures for the total number of in-sourcing authorizations. In a chart showing the distribution of in-sourcing across different DOD components, it gives the total as 16,782. In the data contained in the report listing each component's in-sourcing actions, the total adds to 16,775.

[26] As of October 31, 2011, DOD reported that it employed about 790,000 federal civilians. In its annual inventory of contracted services, required under 10 U.S.C. 2330a, DOD reported to Congress that the level of contractor manpower performing services on DOD's behalf during fiscal year 2010 was equivalent to 623,000 full-time employees. We note that our prior work has found limitations in DOD's reporting associated with this inventory. GAO-11-192.

[27] Throughout this report, we refer to the Department of the Navy when including the Marine Corps, and to the Navy when the Marine Corps is excluded.

suborganization, or directorate of each DOD component that made the in-sourcing decision. For example, the Air Force identified whether Air Combat Command, U.S. Air Forces Europe, or another agency within the Air Force made the decision. See figure 2 for the overall distribution of DOD's fiscal year 2010 in-sourcing actions across its components.

**Figure 2: Distribution of Total DOD In-sourcing Actions for Fiscal Year 2010**

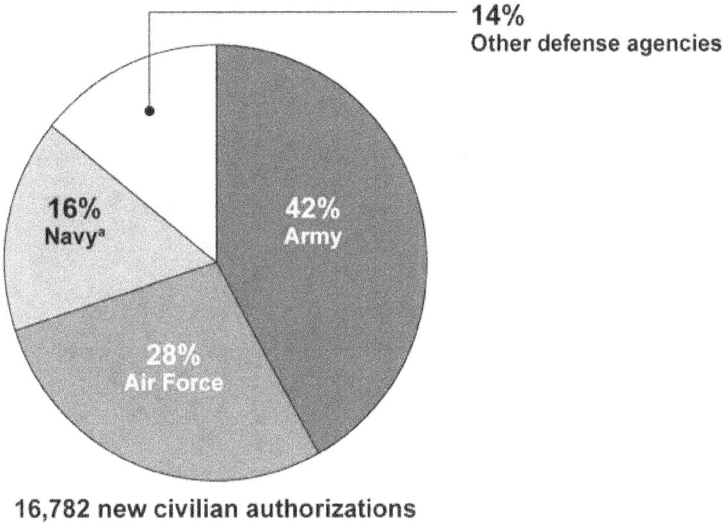

14%
Other defense agencies

16%
Navy[a]

42%
Army

28%
Air Force

**16,782 new civilian authorizations**

Source: GAO analysis of DOD data.

[a] Department of the Navy, including Marine Corps.

## Rationale for In-sourcing

The report also provided information on the rationale for each in-sourcing action across DOD. According to DOD, half of the actions were based on a determination that the function would be more cost effective if performed by DOD civilian employees. While section 323 of the FY11 NDAA did not require DOD to report cost data on in-sourcing, DOD issued guidance in January 2010 on cost estimating methodology for cost-based in-sourcing decisions and the military departments collected and reported some cost estimate data to OUSD (P&R). See appendix II for information on DOD's guidance on estimating in-sourcing costs and collection of cost estimate data.

Additionally, DOD indicated in its September 2011 in-sourcing report to Congress that about 41 percent of the new authorizations would perform functions DOD determined to be exempt from private sector performance, such as those necessary for career progression reasons, continuity of infrastructure operations, or risk mitigation (which included oversight and control of functions that are closely associated with inherently governmental functions). Lastly, DOD reported that about 9 percent of the new authorizations were created to perform work that was determined to be inherently governmental (see fig. 3).

**Figure 3: Reasons DOD Cited for Its Fiscal Year 2010 In-sourcing Decisions**

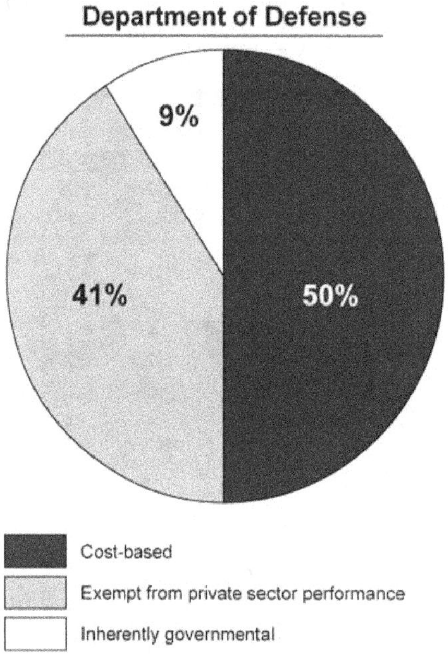

**Department of Defense**

- Cost-based
- Exempt from private sector performance
- Inherently governmental

Source: GAO analysis of DOD data.

Our analysis of the data contained in the DOD in-sourcing report showed that the military services differed in the rationales they cited as the basis for their in-sourcing actions. For example, 86 percent of the Army's new authorizations (5,969 of 6,953) resulting from in-sourcing were deemed exempt from private sector performance in order to reduce the risks associated with contractors performing particular functions that were closely associated with inherently governmental functions. In contrast, 95 percent of the Air Force's new in-sourcing authorizations (4,495 of 4,732) were cost-based and 100 percent of the new Marine Corps authorizations (all 1,042) were cost-based. While the Navy reported that the basis for its fiscal year 2010 in-sourcing actions varied (26 percent or 441 cost-based, 31 percent or 529 inherently governmental, and 43 percent or 716 exempt from private sector performance, out of a total of 1,686), each of the Navy's largest major commands by volume of in-sourcing actions tended to vary as well, with each command citing primarily one basis for its in-sourcing actions which differed among commands. For example, Naval Sea Systems Command reported that its in-sourcing actions largely involved functions considered exempt from private sector performance for career progression reasons, while Pacific Fleet Command in-sourced 223 out of 224 positions for cost reasons. See figure 4 for the distribution of the reasons cited for in-sourcing for each military service.

**Figure 4: Reasons Cited by the Military Services as Reported to Congress**

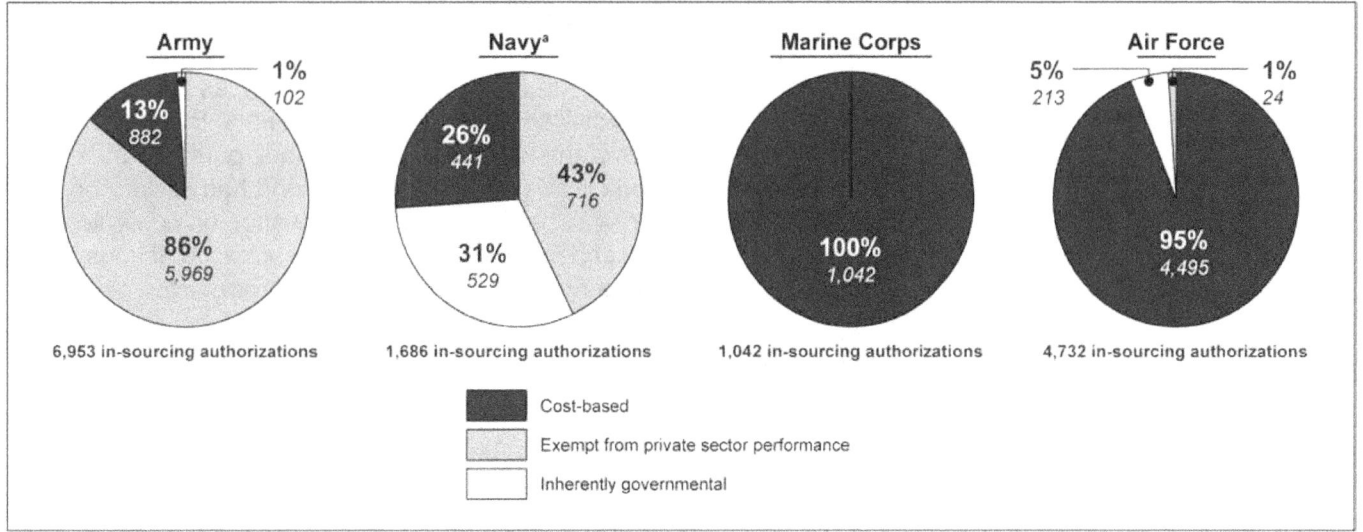

Source: GAO analysis of DOD data.

Note: Numbers may not add due to rounding.

[a] Navy data are as reported to Congress and include errors in certain Navy command data, which we discuss in this report.

OUSD (P&R) and military service officials told us these differences reflect the specific missions and functions of commands and differences in the emphases of military services in the in-sourcing process. For example, Army officials told us that the Army chose to in-source a large number of functions which were closely associated with inherently governmental functions to reduce risk associated with having contractors perform that work. By contrast, Air Force officials told us that they gave "special consideration" to in-sourcing functions closely associated with inherently governmental, however, because the Air Force had sufficient in-house capability in place to oversee the contracted work and could continue contracting for those functions, the Air Force performed costs estimates and in-sourced these functions for cost reasons. Under DOD's implementation of section 2463 of title 10 of the U.S. Code, even though a function is identified as closely associated with inherently governmental, unless that function meets DOD's exempt criteria, the function may only be in-sourced if a cost savings will result.[28]

Furthermore, our work found that differences in the reasons cited for the in-sourcing actions were, in part, due to actions by the military services and major commands to focus their efforts on different objectives when identifying contracts for possible in-sourcing. For example, Air Force and Marine Corps command officials we met with indicated that their objective was to realize cost savings from in-sourcing in order to live within the budget reductions associated with the DOD Comptroller's April 2009 budget decision, which cut funds from contracted services and placed a portion of those funds in civilian authorizations accounts. By contrast, officials of Naval Sea Systems Command told us they pursued an in-sourcing process based on an analysis the command had performed of weaknesses in its internal capabilities and over-reliance on contactors, and this resulted in categorizing the command's in-sourcing actions as exempt from private sector performance for career progression reasons. Similarly, at one Army command, officials we met with in-sourced mainly due to a statutory requirement that security guards on military bases be government civilians.

DOD's in-sourcing report further noted that in-sourcing has been an effective tool for the department to rebalance its workforce, realign inherently governmental and other critical work to government performance, and in many cases, generate resource efficiencies for higher priority goals.

## DOD Did Not Provide the Number of Contractor Employees Whose Functions Were In-sourced

DOD's in-sourcing report did not provide the number of contractor employees whose functions were in-sourced as required, stating that the department did not report this information because the department does not directly employ or hire individual contractor employees. DOD further stated that the department contracts for services to be performed, so the number of employees used to perform these services is not a decision of the department but is at the discretion of the contractor. The report also

---

[28] Deputy Secretary of Defense, *In-Sourcing Contracted Services-Implementation Guidance* (May 28, 2009).

stated that the department's in-sourcing actions are focused on services and not individual contractor positions or employees.

OUSD (P&R) officials told us that DOD focuses on contracting for services rather than the number of contractor employees providing these services. OUSD (P&R) officials further noted that the department does not currently have complete information on the number of full-time equivalents of contractor employees providing services to the department. We recognize that the manner in which the service will be performed under the contract is often a decision of the contractor. However, the level of contractor personnel required to perform each activity is a key component of total workforce management. As previously noted, section 2330a of title 10 of the U.S. Code requires DOD to submit to Congress an annual inventory of all activities performed pursuant to contracts for services and data associated with each activity to include the number of contractor employees, expressed as full-time equivalents, based on the number of direct labor hours and associated cost data collected from contractors, paid for performance of the contracted services.[29] Our prior work has found that DOD faces limitations in obtaining or estimating this information.[30] For example, we found that the federal government's primary data system for tracking information on contracting actions does not provide all the data elements required for the inventory of contracted services. Though DOD has submitted four annual inventories to Congress, as noted in our prior work, with the exception of the Army's inventory data, the information in the DOD inventories is largely derived from databases that do not collect the information required by section 2330a of title 10 of the U.S. Code. In its September 2011 in-sourcing report to Congress, DOD noted that ongoing efforts to collect the information required by section 2330a may in the future help inform the number of contractor full-time equivalents in-sourced. In November 2011 DOD submitted to Congress a plan to collect personnel data directly from contractors. According to this plan, DOD will institute a phased-in approach to do so by fiscal year 2016.

---

[29] Title 10, U.S.C. Section 2330a (c) (E) (2010).

[30] GAO-11-192.

## DOD and Military Department Approaches to Verifying Reported Data Varied

To produce the report on fiscal year 2010 in-sourcing actions, OUSD (P&R) requested that DOD components provide certain information about their fiscal year 2010 in-sourcing actions, and DOD and the military departments took varying, and in some instances limited, approaches to ensuring the reliability of the reported data. For example, the Air Force required major commands to certify the accuracy of the data they reported to Air Force headquarters, while the Navy also delegated responsibility for ensuring data reliability to its major commands but did not establish a policy requiring data certifications. GAO's *Standards for Internal Control in the Federal Government* states that internal controls, which include verifications and edit checks, help provide management with reasonable assurance that agencies have achieved their objectives, including compliance with applicable laws and regulations and the reliability of financial and other internal and external reports.[31]

## Process of Collecting Report Data

To obtain data for the report, OUSD (P&R) sent a reporting template to DOD components which requested the following information:

- the name of the component,
- major command/suborganization/directorate,
- location,
- in-sourcing rationale,
- estimated annual savings,
- DOD function code,[32]
- occupational series,[33]
- whether the position was filled,
- whether it was part of the defense acquisition workforce, and
- whether the action had a small business impact.

OUSD (P&R) included a subset of this information in the September 2011 in-sourcing report to Congress, including the component, major command/suborganization/directorate, location, rationale, and function code.

---

[31] GAO/AIMD-00-21.3.1.

[32] DOD function codes describe work performed in the defense infrastructure and operating forces in direct support of military and civil works missions.

[33] Occupational series codes describe positions with similar specialized line of work and qualification requirements.

To provide the data, both the Air Force and the Department of the Navy obtained data from their respective major commands, while the Army compiled its in-sourcing data at the headquarters level using several data sources originally populated by major commands. The major commands we met with in the Air Force and the Department of the Navy—like the Army headquarters—used various information systems and other sources in compiling their in-sourcing data, since no one data source could provide all the information required. These data sources included personnel databases such as the Defense Civilian Personnel Data System as well as service-specific personnel systems, and the results of reviews of contracts and inventories of contracted services, among other sources.

## Data Validation

The Air Force required major commands to certify the accuracy of the data they reported to Air Force headquarters on each in-sourcing action. More specifically, the guidance required reviews and certifications by key personnel—including reviews by personnel, contracting, finance, and manpower officials.[34] The guidance included a worksheet which required certifications of all the data contained in the business case analyses which were required for each in-sourcing action. Air Force officials told us that the data contained in the business case analyses were used by major commands to generate the reports on in-sourcing actions submitted by the major commands to Air Force headquarters.

The Department of the Navy also delegated responsibility for ensuring data reliability to its major commands, though it did not establish a certification requirement or issue other guidance to help ensure the reliability of the in-sourcing data it collected and reported to OUSD (P&R) for the in-sourcing report to Congress. Army headquarters officials told us that they had established a general level of accuracy in the in-sourcing data by cross-checking three databases in order to produce the data reported to OUSD (P&R), and by sending the personnel data to major commands to cross-check with reviews of contracted services. However, Army headquarters officials told us only a limited number of commands responded to this data request in time to include their checks in the submission to OUSD (P&R). Army officials told us the department did not

---

[34] Air Force, *Air Force Checklist: In-Sourcing Procedures Guide (Using DTM_COMPARE35 to Perform Costing in Accordance with DTM 09-007)* (Mar. 17, 2010).

establish a formal mechanism or issue guidance to ensure the reliability of the in-sourcing data it reported to OUSD (P&R), but Army headquarters officials told us that although the in-sourcing data they reported was not of auditable accuracy, it generally reflected commands' in-sourcing actions.

At the OSD level, OUSD (P&R) officials told us that due to time and resource constraints, they did not verify or validate the in-sourcing data they collected beyond checking for obvious errors such as omissions, and performing cross-checks with data from the department's inventory of inherently governmental and commercial activities. Where disconnects were identified, an OUSD (P&R) official told us they went back to the DOD components for correction of inconsistencies. However, the official told us that there is no mechanism at the OSD level to verify the accuracy of components' data, and that this limitation on data verification exists for all activities in the department, not just in-sourcing. OUSD (P&R) officials told us that DOD intentionally pursued a decentralized in-sourcing process to reduce bureaucratic procedures that would have limited commands' abilities to make timely in-sourcing decisions.

Our work identified either an inaccuracy in the information reported to OUSD (P&R) for the in-sourcing report or concerns about the accuracy of the data included in the report to Congress at four of the nine major commands we met with, as the following examples illustrate:

- The Navy's Fleet Forces Command acknowledged that while they reported establishing 348 authorizations (out of a total of 354 fiscal year 2010 in-sourcing authorizations) to perform information technology functions that were inherently governmental, these authorizations should have been categorized as exempt from private sector performance for continuity of infrastructure operations.[35] Similarly, Space and Naval Warfare Systems Command officials told us that 130 of their reported 131 total fiscal year 2010 in-sourcing authorizations that were identified as inherently governmental were actually in-sourced for career progression reasons.
- Army Medical Command officials told us they did not believe that the data submitted by the Army for DOD's in-sourcing report accurately

---

[35] These actions were associated with the Navy's efforts to upgrade the Navy/Marine Corps Intranet. For additional information on these efforts, see GAO, *Information Technology: Better Informed Decision Making Needed on Navy's Next Generation Enterprise Network Acquisition*, GAO-11-150 (Washington, D.C.: Mar. 11, 2011).

indicated the correct number of new authorizations as a result of in-sourcing by Army Medical Command in fiscal year 2010. Command officials told us that because command staff did not have a consistent understanding of when a new authorization fit the definition of in-sourcing, in some cases new authorizations were coded as in-sourcing when they should not have been, and in other cases new in-sourcing authorizations were not coded as such. The officials said that as a result, the data Army headquarters drew on to compile the in-sourcing data contained both under- and over-reporting of in-sourcing actions. Nevertheless, they said they believed the data, though not precisely accurate, reflected the scale of in-sourcing activity at the command in fiscal year 2010.

The need for accurate data is not unique to in-sourcing decisions. GAO's *Standards for Internal Control in the Federal Government* states that internal controls, which include verifications and edit checks, help provide management with reasonable assurance that agencies have achieved their objectives, including compliance with applicable laws and regulations and the reliability of financial and other internal and external reports.[36] Without access to accurate data, decision makers in DOD and Congress may not have reliable information to help manage and oversee DOD's in-sourcing actions.

## Alignment between In-sourcing Actions and Strategic Workforce Plans Is Unclear

While section 323 of the FY11 NDAA did not require the in-sourcing report to address whether DOD's fiscal year 2010 in-sourcing actions aligned with the department's strategic workforce plans, DOD officials told us that the department had taken some initial steps to align these efforts. Further, DOD officials indicated that DOD's fiscal year 2010 in-sourcing efforts were generally consistent with the department's strategic workforce objectives. DOD's in-sourcing implementation guidance required components to identify contracted services for possible in-sourcing as part of a total force approach to strategic human capital planning, and we and the Office of Personnel Management have identified aligning an organization's human capital program with its current and emerging mission and programmatic goals as a critical need

---

[36] GAO/AIMD-00-21.3.1.

of strategic workforce planning.[37] However, differences in the types of data used in the in-sourcing report and workforce plans hinder an accurate assessment of the degree to which DOD's use of in-sourcing achieved the department's strategic workforce objectives.

With respect to the steps DOD took to align in-sourcing with its strategic workforce plans, the department identified a goal for the in-sourcing initiative in its March 2010 civilian strategic workforce plan. The plan stated that the goal was to optimize the department's workforce mix to maintain readiness and operational capability, ensure inherently governmental positions were performed by government employees, and construct the workforce in an effective, cost efficient manner. In addition, OUSD (P&R) officials noted that they had convened an in-sourcing "community of interest" in 2009 to prepare DOD's functional communities for the fiscal year 2010 in-sourcing efforts, and briefed DOD component functional community managers on the in-sourcing process. OUSD (P&R) officials responsible for strategic workforce planning and the report on fiscal year 2010 in-sourcing actions told us, however, that they had not established metrics to measure progress toward the stated goal of the in-sourcing effort, and acknowledged that it would be difficult to measure such progress from the available data.

Further, DOD officials indicated that because DOD uses different identifiers for workforce planning efforts than it does to track in-sourcing actions, DOD does not have the ability to correlate the underlying data. For example, DOD's most recent strategic workforce plans used occupational series codes—representing occupations such as budget analyst (0560) or civil engineer (0810)—while the in-sourcing report used function codes, which describe a broad area of work such as logistics or intelligence.[38] DOD officials told us there is no crosswalk between occupational series and function codes, and one occupational series can be found in many different function codes—for example, a budget analyst could work in logistics or professional military education, among other

---

[37] GAO, *Human Capital: Key Principles for Effective Strategic Workforce Planning*, GAO-04-39 (Washington, D.C.: Dec. 11, 2003) and *Workforce Planning: Interior, EPA, and the Forest Service Should Strengthen Linkages to Their Strategic Plans and Improve Evaluation*, GAO-10-413 (Washington, D.C.: Mar. 31, 2010).

[38] DOD, *Strategic Civilian Human Capital Plan (SCHCP) 2006-2010, Fiscal Year 2009 status report* (Mar. 31, 2010), and *DOD Strategic Human Capital Plan Update, The Defense Acquisition Workforce* (April 2010).

functions. Though they were not published in the report to Congress, the data military departments reported to OUSD (P&R) included occupational series, but those data are limited in the extent to which they can be used to measure progress against the strategic workforce plans. For example, the non-acquisition workforce plans did not contain specific workforce targets for in-sourcing. Similarly, the acquisition workforce plan did not contain workforce targets by occupational series, but instead outlined targets for increasing acquisition career fields, which consist of many, overlapping occupational series. For example, four different career fields—including the "test and evaluation" and "production, quality & manufacturing" career fields—contain the general engineer (0801) occupation. Thus, the data components provided to OUSD (P&R) for the in-sourcing report also could not be used to compare with the in-sourcing targets contained in the acquisition community workforce plan.

DOD officials stated that they believe the department's fiscal year 2010 in-sourcing actions were consistent with the broad goals outlined in their 2010 workforce plans, and had the effect of freeing up funds for higher-priority areas because of cost efficiencies, and of reducing risks associated with contractors performing inherently governmental or closely associated with inherently governmental functions. However, without greater alignment between the in-sourcing data and strategic workforce plans, decision makers in DOD and Congress have limited information about the extent to which in-sourcing actions furthered the department's strategic workforce goals.

## Conclusions

In-sourcing is one tool DOD can use to balance its workforce mix among DOD civilians, military personnel, and contractors to help ensure it has the right balance of in-house capabilities to perform its mission and reduce the risk of over-reliance on its contractor workforce. DOD stated in its September 2011 report to Congress that its fiscal year 2010 in-sourcing decisions helped the department achieve these objectives. DOD reported on its fiscal year 2010 in-sourcing actions as Congress required, listing the creation of nearly 17,000 new civilian authorizations as a result of in-sourcing by DOD components. The report also listed the DOD component taking the in-sourcing action and the basis and rationale for each action. However, DOD and the military departments took only limited steps to ensure that the report data, such as the number of new in-sourcing authorizations in each command and the stated rationale for the actions, were reliable. In some instances, we found the data submitted by the major commands to be inaccurate due to insufficient mechanisms for validating the reliability of the data. Without greater assurance of data reliability, the report itself, as well as any data DOD may continue to collect on its ongoing in-sourcing actions in the future, may have limited utility as a tool to facilitate oversight by decision makers in both DOD and Congress. Likewise, the data collected on in-sourcing could not be used to measure progress toward the department's overall goal for its in-sourcing initiative according to its strategic workforce plans. The lack of alignment between strategic-level workforce plans and the fiscal year 2010 in-sourcing data and the lack of metrics to measure progress against strategic workforce objectives limits decision makers' insight into the extent to which in-sourcing in fiscal year 2010 strengthened the DOD workforce in key areas.

## Recommendations for Executive Action

To address these issues, we recommend that the Secretary of Defense take the following two actions:

To enhance insights into and facilitate oversight of the department's in-sourcing efforts, we recommend that the Secretary of Defense direct the Under Secretary of Defense for Personnel and Readiness to issue guidance to DOD components requiring that the components establish a process to help ensure the accuracy of any data collected on future in-sourcing decisions.

To improve DOD's strategic workforce planning, we recommend that the Secretary of Defense direct the Under Secretary of Defense for Personnel and Readiness to better align the data collected on in-sourcing with the department's strategic workforce plans and establish metrics with which to measure progress in meeting any in-sourcing goals.

## Agency Comments and Our Evaluation

In commenting on a draft of this report, DOD partially concurred with our two recommendations. DOD's comments are reprinted in appendix III.

In written comments, DOD stated that there was nothing technically incorrect with our statements and findings. DOD noted that in-sourcing is one of many tools managers can use to shape the department's workforce, and has enabled managers throughout the department to enhance internal capabilities, regain control and oversight of mission-critical functions, mitigate risks associated with over-reliance on contracted services, and generate efficiencies through resource realignment. DOD also stated, however, that the department was concerned that the challenges and problems identified in our report were not solely unique or attributable to in-sourcing, and that a lack of clarification on this point might unfairly cast unwarranted criticism on the use of in-sourcing as a tool available to government managers. We agree, and have noted in our report that the need for reliable data is not unique to in-sourcing decisions. However, while the challenges identified in our report regarding data reliability and alignment of reported data with strategic workforce plans may not be unique to in-sourcing, they can pose problems for evaluating the effects of in-sourcing as a tool for workforce management.

DOD partially concurred with our first recommendation, to require components to establish a process to ensure the accuracy of in-sourcing data collected going forward. DOD stated that the challenges to data accuracy identified in our report are not unique to manpower requirements and billets established as a result of in-sourcing contracted services, adding that because the challenges are not unique to in-sourcing, they should not call into question the fundamental value and efficacy of in-sourcing. Our report does not call the value of in-sourcing into question. However, we believe that despite challenges to the accuracy of DOD data in other areas, reliable data on in-sourcing are necessary for oversight by decision makers in DOD and Congress. The department also noted that because time-sensitive in-sourcing decisions must often be made at the command or installation level, any certification and validation process should occur at that level. We agree and, as we stated in our recommendation, believe that the department should require that components establish a process to help ensure the accuracy of in-sourcing data, which does not preclude certification and validation by commands or installations.

DOD also partially concurred with our second recommendation, to better align the data collected on in-sourcing with the department's strategic workforce plans and establish metrics with which to measure progress in meeting any in-sourcing goals. The department stated that it has worked to align in-sourcing and strategic workforce planning efforts and that in-sourcing is one of many tools available to help close competency gaps and meet strategic workforce planning goals. However, the department further stated that in-sourcing should not be limited to areas identified in strategic workforce plans. We do not suggest in our report that in-sourcing should be limited to areas identified in strategic workforce plans, but believe that the effect that in-sourcing has in helping to achieve strategic workforce goals should be identified and reported as part of the oversight of the department's strategic workforce management. DOD further stated that objectively measuring in-sourcing outcomes with traditional workload or personnel metrics is challenging because of unique, location-specific conditions related to missions, functions, and operating environments. In that regard, as we state in our report, DOD officials acknowledged that they had not established metrics to measure progress against the in-sourcing goal in the department's most recent strategic workforce plan and that it would be difficult to use the available data to assess such progress. However, as our prior work has noted, a key principle of strategic workforce planning is monitoring and evaluating progress toward human capital goals.[39] We note that without any metrics and measurements indicating the extent to which in-sourcing helped the department make progress toward strategic workforce goals, decision makers in DOD and Congress will be unable to assess the effect of the department's in-sourcing actions in comparison with other actions it may take to manage the size and composition of the total workforce.

We are sending copies of this report to appropriate congressional committees, the Secretary of Defense, and other interested parties. In addition, the report will be available at no charge on the GAO website at http://www.gao.gov.

If you or your staff have any questions concerning this report, please contact us at (202) 512-3604 or farrellb@gao.gov, or (202) 512-4841 or martinb@gao.gov. Contact points for our Offices of Congressional Relations and Public Affairs may be found on the last page of this report. Key contributors to this report are listed in appendix IV.

Brenda S. Farrell
Director, Defense Capabilities and Management

Belva M. Martin
Director, Acquisition and Sourcing Management

---

[39] GAO-04-39.

*List of Committees*

The Honorable Carl Levin
Chairman
The Honorable John McCain
Ranking Member
Committee on Armed Services
United States Senate

The Honorable Daniel Inouye
Chairman
The Honorable Thad Cochran
Ranking Member
Subcommittee on Defense
Committee on Appropriations
United States Senate

The Honorable Howard "Buck" McKeon
Chairman
The Honorable Adam Smith
Ranking Member
Committee on Armed Services
House of Representatives

The Honorable C.W. Bill Young
Chairman
The Honorable Norman D. Dicks
Ranking Member
Subcommittee on Defense
Committee on Appropriations
House of Representatives

# Appendix I: Scope and Methodology

To evaluate the extent to which the Department of Defense (DOD) reported on the items required by section 323 of the National Defense Authorization Act (NDAA) for Fiscal Year 2011, we reviewed DOD's report on its fiscal year 2010 in-sourcing actions and compared it with the items specifically required by the legislation. Specifically, we ascertained the extent to which DOD reported on: (1) the agency or service of the department involved in the decision, (2) the basis and rationale for the decision, and (3) the number of contractor employees whose functions were converted to performance by DOD civilians. To better understand the data DOD reported, we reviewed DOD guidance on the in-sourcing decision-making process as well as statutes and regulations relating to in-sourcing, and met with officials of the Office of the Under Secretary of Defense for Personnel and Readiness (OUSD (P&R)) responsible for preparing the report, as well as officials in the departments of the Army, Navy, and Air Force responsible for submitting data for the report to OUSD (P&R). We focused our work on the military departments because together they constituted the majority of in-sourcing actions in fiscal year 2010. We analyzed the data contained in the report to identify patterns in the in-sourcing actions of the military departments, and met with representatives of each military department and the selected major commands to identify the reasons for those patterns. We used these data to portray the distribution of in-sourcing actions across the military departments and other DOD agencies, as well as the distribution of in-sourcing rationales in the military services and within certain major commands. For the purposes of this review, we selected a non-probability sample of commands from each military service, which included at a minimum the largest two commands in each service by volume of in-sourcing actions in fiscal year 2010. The sample of commands is not generalizable to all military department major commands.

To determine the process DOD used to prepare the report and the extent to which the department assured itself of the reliability of the data, we reviewed our prior work on standards for internal control in the federal government.[1] We also reviewed DOD guidance on the in-sourcing decision process. We analyzed the data contained in DOD's report to identify patterns in the in-sourcing actions of the military departments, and met with officials of OUSD (P&R) in charge of preparing the report, as

---

[1] GAO, *Standards for Internal Control in the Federal Government*, GAO/AIMD-00-21.3.1 (Washington, D.C.: November 1999).

well as officials in the three military departments responsible for submitting in-sourcing data to OUSD (P&R), to identify the reasons for those patterns. As previously noted, we focused our work on the military departments because together they constituted the majority of in-sourcing actions in fiscal year 2010. We obtained and reviewed the in-sourcing data submitted by the military departments, and compared these data to the data in the report submitted to Congress. We also met with select major commands to determine their processes for assuring the reliability of the data they generated on in-sourcing actions, as well as certain other major commands with significant in-sourcing actions. We did not independently verify the data submitted for use in the report. We used these data to portray the distribution of in-sourcing actions across the military departments and other DOD agencies, as well as the distribution of in-sourcing rationales in the military services and within certain major commands. Although we found problems with some of the command-level data and are making a recommendation to this effect, we found the data to be sufficiently reliable for the purposes of providing broad percentages about in-sourcing actions.

To determine the extent to which DOD's fiscal year 2010 in-sourcing actions were aligned with the department's recent strategic workforce plans, we reviewed our and the Office of Personnel Management's prior work on strategic workforce planning. We compared the data in the report on fiscal year 2010 in-sourcing actions and in-sourcing data submitted by the three military departments with the department's most recent strategic workforce plans (specifically, the 2009 update to the 2006-2010 strategic workforce plans). We also interviewed officials in OUSD (P&R) responsible for preparing both the in-sourcing report and the strategic workforce plans, and officials in the Office of the Under Secretary of Defense for Acquisition, Technology, and Logistics' Office of Human Capital Initiatives responsible for the acquisition community's strategic workforce plans.

DOD organizations we contacted during audit work included the following:

In the Office of the Secretary of Defense:

- Office of the Under Secretary of Defense (Personnel & Readiness)
- Office of the Under Secretary of Defense (Comptroller)
- Office of the Under Secretary of Defense (Acquisition, Technology, and Logistics)

In the Department of the Air Force:

- Office of the Assistant Secretary of the Air Force (Manpower & Reserve Affairs)
- Headquarters Air Force
- Air Force Materiel Command

In the Department of the Army:

- Office of the Assistant Secretary of the Army (Manpower & Reserve Affairs)
- Army Installation Management Command
- Army Medical Command

In the Department of the Navy:

- Office of the Assistant Secretary of the Navy (Manpower & Reserve Affairs)
- Office of the Chief of Naval Operations
- Headquarters Marine Corps
- Navy Fleet Forces Command
- Naval Sea Systems Command
- Space and Naval Warfare Systems Command
- Marine Corps Systems Command

We conducted this performance audit from May 2011 to February 2012 in accordance with generally accepted government auditing standards. Those standards require that we plan and perform the audit to obtain sufficient, appropriate evidence to provide a reasonable basis for our findings and conclusions based on our audit objectives.

# Appendix II: DOD Cost Estimating Guidance and Cost Estimate Data Collection

While section 323 of the FY11 NDAA did not require DOD to report cost data on in-sourcing and DOD's September 2011 report to Congress did not include any cost-related information, DOD issued guidance to components on the methodology to use when making cost-based in-sourcing decisions,[1] and the military departments collected and reported estimated cost information on their respective in-sourcing actions to varying degrees.

## Guidance on In-sourcing Cost Estimates

DOD's May 2009 in-sourcing guidance requires DOD components, in the case of work which is not determined to be inherently governmental or exempt from private sector performance and which can be performed by DOD civilians, to conduct a cost analysis to determine whether DOD civilian employees or the private sector would be the most cost-effective provider. In January 2010, DOD issued guidance on the methodology components should use to estimate the costs of in-sourcing actions when making cost-based in-sourcing decisions. Officials in the military departments told us that although the guidance was officially released in January 2010, the costing rules were available previously and so were used throughout fiscal year 2010.

## Collecting and Reporting Cost Data

We found that the military departments took different approaches to collecting and reporting cost-related data associated with their fiscal year 2010 in-sourcing decisions. Specifically, the Air Force collected and reported cost estimate data for each in-sourcing action—including cost-based, inherently governmental, and exempt functions—to OUSD (P&R). The Department of the Navy collected and reported cost estimate data to OUSD (P&R) for most cost-based in-sourcing actions and some actions that were not cost-based. Specifically, the Navy reported cost estimate data on some, but not all, in-sourcing actions for functions that were deemed inherently governmental or exempt from private sector

---

[1] DOD, *Directive-Type Memorandum (DTM) 09-007, "Estimating and Comparing the Full Costs of Civilian and Military Manpower and Contract Support"* (Jan. 29, 2010, updated Oct. 21, 2010).

performance. The Army did not report any estimated cost data for in-sourcing decisions to OUSD (P&R).[2]

---

[2] As noted previously, the Air Force's new in-sourcing authorizations were 95 percent cost based, while the Department of the Navy's were 54 percent cost based (including the Marine Corps, which in-sourced 100 percent for cost reasons), and the Army's were 13 percent cost based.

# Appendix III: Comments from the Department of Defense

OFFICE OF THE UNDER SECRETARY OF DEFENSE
4000 DEFENSE PENTAGON
WASHINGTON, DC 20301-4000

JAN 27 2012

PERSONNEL AND
READINESS

MEMORANDUM FOR ASSISTANT INSPECTOR GENERAL, COMMUNICATIONS AND
CONGRESSIONAL LIAISON, OFFICE OF THE INSPECTOR
GENERAL, DEPARTMENT OF DEFENSE

SUBJECT: GAO Draft Report, GAO-12-319, "Defense Workforce: DOD Needs to
Better Oversee In-sourcing Data and Align In-sourcing Efforts with Human Capital
Plans"

　　　Attached is DoD's response to subject report. Should you have any questions, please
contact my primary action officer, Mr. Thomas Hessel, Associate Director of Total Force
Requirements and Sourcing Policy, at 703-697-3402, or at thomas.hessel@osd.mil.

Sincerely,

P. M. Tamburrino
Deputy Assistant Secretary of Defense
Civilian Personnel Policy

Attachments:
As stated

OFFICE OF THE UNDER SECRETARY OF DEFENSE
4000 DEFENSE PENTAGON
WASHINGTON, DC 20301-4000

PERSONNEL AND
READINESS

Jan 27, 2012

Ms. Brenda Farrell
Director, Defense Capabilities and Management
U.S. Government Accountability Office
441 G Street, N.W.
Washington, DC 20548

Dear Ms. Farrell,

This is the Department of Defense (DoD) response to the GAO draft report 12-319, "Defense Workforce: DOD Needs to Better Oversee In-sourcing Data and Align In-sourcing Efforts with Human Capital Plans".

The Department appreciates the opportunity to review and comment on this draft report. We found nothing technically incorrect with the statements and findings of the GAO. However, the Department is concerned the challenges and problems identified are not solely unique or attributable to in-sourcing. A lack of clarification on this point may unfairly cast unwarranted criticism on the use of in-sourcing as a tool available to government managers.

In-sourcing is one of many tools available to managers to shape the workforce. Throughout the Department, it enables managers to enhance internal capabilities, regain control and oversight of mission critical functions, mitigate risks associated with overreliance on contracted services, and generate efficiencies through resource realignment. However, because of unique, location specific conditions related to missions, functions, and operating environments, objectively measuring such outcomes with traditional workload or personnel metrics is challenging.

As related to the two specific recommendations offered by the GAO, the Department response is as follows:

RECOMMENDATION 1: The GAO recommends that the Secretary of Defense direct the Under Secretary of Defense for Personnel and Readiness to issue guidance to DoD components requiring that the components establish a process to help ensure the accuracy of any data collected on future in-sourcing decisions.

DoD RESPONSE: The Department partially concurs with this recommendation. The challenges related to data accuracy are not unique to manpower requirements and billets established as a result of in-sourcing contracted services. Additionally, the Department faces challenges very similar to the ones identified in GAO's report. These challenges are not unique to in-sourcing; therefore, they should not call into question the fundamental value and efficacy of in-sourcing. Steps to improve overall Total Force management, application of manpower mix criteria, and appropriate documentation of manpower requirements are underway across the Department. While not exclusive to in-sourcing, these actions are a part of a broader effort to improve visibility, accountability, and management of the Total Force; they include the following areas: the Inherently Governmental/Commercial Activities Inventory; the Inventory of Contracts for Services; and the Programming, Planning, and Budget process. Because time-sensitive in-sourcing decisions to ensure the right mix to meet mission requirements must often be made at the command or installation level, any certification and validation process should occur at that level.

**RECOMMENDATION 2**: The GAO recommends that the Secretary of Defense direct the Under Secretary of Defense for Personnel and Readiness to better align the data collected on in-sourcing with the Department's strategic workforce plans and establish metrics with which to measure progress in meeting any in-sourcing goals.

**DoD RESPONSE**: The Department partially concurs with this recommendation. The Department has worked to align in-sourcing and strategic workforce planning efforts. The strategic workforce plan addresses the extent to which competency gaps exist and outlines gap closure strategies. In-sourcing is one of many tools available to managers to help close these gaps and meet strategic workforce planning goals. However, in-sourcing is a tool for managers to shape the entire workforce and should not be limited solely to those functional or occupational areas identified in the strategic workforce plans. Additionally, establishing metrics solely for the purposes of documenting progress against in-sourcing goals must be appropriately developed to properly gauge the efficacy of plans to maintain a balanced, capable workforce vice strictly in-sourcing goals.

In-sourcing has been, and continues to be, a very effective tool for the Department to rebalance the workforce, realign inherently governmental and other critical work to government performance (from contract support), and in many instances to generate resource efficiencies.

Should you have any questions, please contact my primary action officer Mr. Thomas Hessel, Associate Director of Total Force Requirements and Sourcing Policy, at 703-697-3402, or at thomas.hessel@osd.mil.

Sincerely,

P. M. Tamburrino
Deputy Assistant Secretary of Defense
Civilian Personnel Policy

# Appendix IV: GAO Contacts and Staff Acknowledgments

| | |
|---|---|
| **GAO Contacts** | Brenda S. Farrell, (202) 512-3604 or farrellb@gao.gov.<br><br>Belva M. Martin, (202) 512-4841 or martinb@gao.gov. |
| **Staff Acknowledgments** | In addition to the contacts named above, key contributors to this report were Marion Gatling, Assistant Director; Randy DeLeon; Tim DiNapoli, Simon Hirschfeld; John Krump; Ramzi Nemo; Terry Richardson; and Erik Wilkins-McKee. |

| | |
|---|---|
| **GAO's Mission** | The Government Accountability Office, the audit, evaluation, and investigative arm of Congress, exists to support Congress in meeting its constitutional responsibilities and to help improve the performance and accountability of the federal government for the American people. GAO examines the use of public funds; evaluates federal programs and policies; and provides analyses, recommendations, and other assistance to help Congress make informed oversight, policy, and funding decisions. GAO's commitment to good government is reflected in its core values of accountability, integrity, and reliability. |
| **Obtaining Copies of GAO Reports and Testimony** | The fastest and easiest way to obtain copies of GAO documents at no cost is through GAO's website (www.gao.gov). Each weekday afternoon, GAO posts on its website newly released reports, testimony, and correspondence. To have GAO e-mail you a list of newly posted products, go to www.gao.gov and select "E-mail Updates." |
| **Order by Phone** | The price of each GAO publication reflects GAO's actual cost of production and distribution and depends on the number of pages in the publication and whether the publication is printed in color or black and white. Pricing and ordering information is posted on GAO's website, http://www.gao.gov/ordering.htm. <br><br>Place orders by calling (202) 512-6000, toll free (866) 801-7077, or TDD (202) 512-2537. <br><br>Orders may be paid for using American Express, Discover Card, MasterCard, Visa, check, or money order. Call for additional information. |
| **Connect with GAO** | Connect with GAO on Facebook, Flickr, Twitter, and YouTube. Subscribe to our RSS Feeds or E-mail Updates. Listen to our Podcasts. Visit GAO on the web at www.gao.gov. |
| **To Report Fraud, Waste, and Abuse in Federal Programs** | Contact: <br><br>Website: www.gao.gov/fraudnet/fraudnet.htm <br>E-mail: fraudnet@gao.gov <br>Automated answering system: (800) 424-5454 or (202) 512-7470 |
| **Congressional Relations** | Katherine Siggerud, Managing Director, siggerudk@gao.gov, (202) 512-4400, U.S. Government Accountability Office, 441 G Street NW, Room 7125, Washington, DC 20548 |
| **Public Affairs** | Chuck Young, Managing Director, youngc1@gao.gov, (202) 512-4800 U.S. Government Accountability Office, 441 G Street NW, Room 7149 Washington, DC 20548 |

www.ingramcontent.com/pod-product-compliance
Lightning Source LLC
Chambersburg PA
CBHW080931290526
45795CB00007BA/2702